A devotional by

~~ Linda O'Dell ~~

These pages are full of scriptures used behind the gates! The women were so encouraged & it strengthened their faith. May they minister to you also!

Linda ODell
5-5-2...
Ezekiel 11:25

LIVE!!
Ezekiel 16
{6/26/2001}

v6   Jesus saw us struggling in our own sin, dying
and He said 'LIVE'!!

v7   He made us THRIVE like a plant in a field
we grew and matured.
We became very BEAUTIFUL
but we were naked and bare.

v8   Jesus saw us again and He spread His wing over us
and covered our nakedness.
Jesus entered a covenant with us and swore an oath
Isaiah 43:1 'you became Mine!' says the Lord God.

v9   He WASHED us, ANOINTED us with oil
CLOTHED us in embroidered cloth, fine linen and
silk, gave us sandals for our feet.

v11   He ADORNED us with ornaments of gold and silver
bracelets, chains, earrings and a beautiful crown
He FED us with fine flour, honey and oil
we were exceedingly beautiful, succeeding to
ROYALTY!

v14   God bestowed His splendor on us.....BUT.....

v15   we trusted in our 'own' beauty, played the harlot with
everyone

v16   that passed by. We took our garments and adorned
high places
and entered into pagan worship

v17   we made idols with our beautiful jewelry
v18   set His oil and incense before idols
v19   we gave our fine food to idols as a sweet incense offering
v20   we sacrificed our children to the fire
v22   we forgot our past and where we came from and what God had brought us through
v23   we multiplied our harlotry, made shrines to idols on every street
v24   and made our beauty to be abhorred.
v27   God gave us up to those who hated us, those who were ashamed
v28   still we were not satisfied
v30   *** DEGENERATE is your heart says the Lord
v33   we were worse than others because we paid for those to come to us in our harlotry, instead of getting paid.
v38   God will judge
v39   and strip us leaving us naked and bare
v41   God will make us cease playing the harlot
v47   we were worse than Sodom and Samaria, more abominable
v59   God will deal with us as we broke His covenant
v60   God will remember the covenant that He made with us in our youth and establish an everlasting covenant with us
v63   and we will know that He is the Lord God and we will remember and never open our mouths again because of our shame when He provides ATONEMENT for ALL we have done.
       PRAISE GOD!

Rebellious House

{Instructions for prison ministry from the Bible}
{2001}

Ezekiel chapter 16

Read His word & understand, He said to me, "Son of man, stand on your feet & I will speak to you". Then the Spirit entered me when He spoke to me & set me on my feet.

I HEARD Him who SPOKE to me & He said to me, "Son of man, I am SENDING you to the children of Israel to a REBELLIOUS nation that has rebelled against me.

They & their fathers have transgressed against Me to this very day. For they are impudent & stubborn children. I am sending you to them & you shall say to them whether they hear or whether they refuse for they are a REBELLIOUS HOUSE.

They will know that a prophet has been among them & you son of man, do not be AFRAID of them nor be afraid of their words though briers & thorns are with you & you dwell among scorpions. Do not be afraid of their words or dismayed by their looks though they are a rebellious house.

You shall speak my words to them, whether they hear or whether they refuse for they are a rebellious house. But you, son of man, hear what I say to you. Do not be rebellious like the rebellious house. Open your mouth & eat what I give you. Now when I looked there was a hand stretched out to me & behold a scroll of a book was in it. Then He spread it before me & there was writing on the inside & on the outside & written on it were lamentations, mourning & woe.

Moreover He said to me, "Son of man, eat what you find, eat this scroll & GO & SPEAK to the house of Israel". So I opened my mouth & He caused me to eat that scroll & He said to me, "Son of man, feed your belly & fill your stomach with the scroll that I will give you". So I ate & it was in my mouth like honey in sweetness. Then He said to me, "Son of man, GO to the house of Israel & SPEAK with my words to them for you are not sent to a people of unfamiliar speech & of hard language.

But to the house of Israel, not to many people of unfamiliar speech or hard language whose words you cannot understand. Surely had I sent you to them they would have listened to you but the house of Israel will not listen to you, because they will not listen to me for all the house of Israel are impudent hard hearted. Behold, I have made your face, strong against their faces, your forehead strong against their foreheads, like adament stone harder than flint. I have made your forehead . Do not be afraid of them nor be dismayed at their looks, though they are a rebellious house.

Moreover, He said to me "Son of man, receive into your heart all my words that I speak to you & hear with your ears & GO get to the CAPTIVES, to the children of my people & speak to them & tell them thus says the Lord God whether they hear or whether they refuse." Then the Spirit lifted me up & I heard behind me a great thunderous voice. Blessed is the glory of the Lord from this place.

I also, heard the noise of the wings of the winged creatures that touched one another & the noise of the wheels beside them & a great thunderous noise so the Spirit lifted me up & took me away & I went in bitterness in the heart of my spirit but the hand of the Lord was strong upon me then I came to the captives at Tel Abib who dwelleth by the River Chebar.

& I SAT and remained there ASTONISHED among
them 7 days.
Now it came to past at the end of 7 days that the word of the
Lord came to me saying,"Son of man, I have made you a
WATCHMAN for the house of Israel. Therefore, hear a word
from my mouth & give them warning from me. When I say to
the wicked, "You shall surely die". you give them no warning
nor speak to warn the wicked from his wicked way to save his
life, that same wicked man shall die in his iniquity but his
 blood I will require at your hand.
 Yet if you warn the wicked & he does not turn from his
 wickedness he shall die in his iniquity but you have delivered
 your soul again when a righteous man turns from his
 righteousness & commits iniquity & I lay a stumbling block
 before him, he shall die because you did not give him
 warning, he shall die in his sin & his righteousness which he
 has done shall not be remembered, but his blood I will require
at your hand.
 Nevertheless, if you turn the righteous man that he
 should not sin & he does not sin he shall surely live because
 he took warning & also you have delivered your soul."
Then the hand of the Lord was upon me & He said to me
"Arise & go out into the plain & there I shall talk with you".
 So I arose & went out into the plain & behold the glory of the
 Lord stood there like the glory which I say by the River Chebar
& I fell on my face! The Spirit entered me & set me on my feet
& spoke with me & said to me "Go shut yourself inside your
 house & you son of man, surely they will put ropes on you &
 bind you with them so that you cannot go out among them.

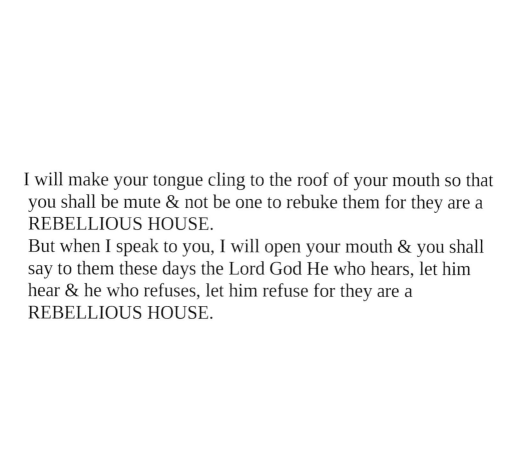

I will make your tongue cling to the roof of your mouth so that you shall be mute & not be one to rebuke them for they are a REBELLIOUS HOUSE.
But when I speak to you, I will open your mouth & you shall say to them these days the Lord God He who hears, let him hear & he who refuses, let him refuse for they are a REBELLIOUS HOUSE.

No Correction!
{2002}

Consider this...

Jeremiah 2:30   In vain, I have chastened your children, they receive 'no correction'. Your sword has devoured prophets like a destroying lion. Why? Because there is no transformation of the Holy Spirit in their hearts.

Job 11:10   If He passes by, imprisons & gathers to judgment, who can hinder Him?

Job 12:14   If He breaks a thing down, it can not be rebuilt if He imprisons a man, there can be no release.

Job 19:7 If I cry out concerning wrong, I am not heard, I cry aloud there is no justice!

Jeremiah 2:17-19 Have you not brought this on yourself in that you have forsaken the Lord your God.

Consider Psalm 103:10 He has not dealt with us according to our sins nor punished us according to our iniquities.

Job 11:6 know therefore that God exacts from you less than your iniquity deserves.

By Jesus you receive mercy & grace through the Cross He paid for your penalty of sin on the Cross.

Offering you a paid in full pardon, but you have to accept His forgiveness surrender all to Him, pardon is a free gift but it's not truly yours until you accept it. Our prison system use to be called a House of Correction' where offenders could receive the 'process of correcting' where their punishment was intended to rehabilitate & improve their lives.

Rehabilitate means to 'restore to a good condition' it was the restoration of someone to a useful place in society Something has gone terribly wrong here. The prison system no longer tries to correct or restore.

It has become a 'warehouse' of humanity where profits are made on the mistakes of others. We are all to blame because as a society we have locked
 them up & thrown away the key.
But when this occurs to your mother, father,
son or daughter? Suddenly there is concern!
They are all someone's loved one. How can we expect
 change & be restored to society if we offer them no
support, programs, education, jobs, skills to help
them once released.
Most offenders will be released and all come to
live next door to you! Don't you want them to be a good member of society by then & not just a criminal released from a cage?
There must be an inner spiritual change in the heart
 for real transformation to occur. We must continue to offer our prisons faith based opportunities to change their negative behavior & mindset, & to heal their wounds & hurts of the past.
So they can be prepared for their future. Jesus Christ has changed many lives behind bars, I have witnessed it, I know He works!
Let's continue to with what works & change what is not working.
Change must come to the system & must start at the top before it can reach the least of these. Churches need to become ex-offender friendly putting their faith in action to love & receive those releasing from prison to provide a wrap around service to them to end the the revolving door on the prison.
We must all receive correction today, then reach out to those
 around us.

Biblical Justice
{2003}

What is Justice?
The quality of being just, fairness, conformity to moral righteousness in action & attitude.
The greatest problem of Jurisprudence is to allow freedom while enforcing order.
Real problem is we are warehousing people instead of doing 'corrections'.
Prisons were intended to be the 'House of Correction' ..to set in place a process of correction; to rehabilitate & improve offenders; to restore to a useful place in society. We are a long way from restoring hurting people to their useful place. In Jeremiah 2:30 ' They receive no correction why? Because there is no transformation of the Holy Spirit in their hearts.
It is God who shuts & opens doors, even prison doors
Job 11:10 if He passes by, imprisons & gathers to judgment then who can hinder Him?
Job 12:14 if He breaks a thing down it cannot be rebuilt, if He imprisons a man there can be no release.
The Bible speaks of Justice 135x.
But Job 11:6 says 'know therefore that God exacts from you less than your iniquity deserves.
Psalm 103:10 says 'He has not dealt with us according to our iniquities. Further study reveals the Bible speaks of
prison 125x
prisoner 40x
pardon 18x

correction 18x
case 36x
acquitted 4x

God IS Justice!!
But He is also mercy, grace & forgiveness & love.
He restores, reconciles, repairs, redeems, rescues,
ransoms, revives.
Jesus Christ is our Judge, Advocate & Defense
All have broken God's laws, our sin separated us from
Him.
God is Holy, He must judge sin, as Judge He pronounced
our death sentence, then as our Defense He sacrificed
Himself on the Cross in our place, taking our punishment
purchased our pardon.
He freely did this out of His great love, no one else ever died
for us, was buried, then rose again from the dead!
Proving He has the power & authority to deliver us &
justify us reconciling us back to Himself.
How do we receive this free pardon? We confess our sins
turn from them then ask Him into our hearts as Savior &
Lord.
Asking for His forgiveness, asking the Holy Spirit to draw us
to Him through conviction so we can turn from sin to Him.
Then obey Him & live for Him.
Walk with Him daily as He leads. There is no other savior
Jesus Christ.
Allow Him to bring correction into your life.

Death Penalty Sins...
{2002}

According to the Old Testament, in the Bible, there are 42 sins worthy of the death penalty. Which ones have you committed?

1. Murder   Genesis 9:6; Exodus 21:12-14, 20, 23;
   Leviticus 24:17-21; Numbers 35:16-34
   Deuteronomy 19

2. Failing to Circumcise Genesis 17:14; Exodus 4:24-25

3. Eating leavened bread during Feast of Unleavened Bread
   Exodus 2:15-19

4. Hitting parents Exodus 21:15

5. Kidnapping Exodus 21:16; Deuteronomy 24:7

6. Cursing parents Exodus 21:17; Leviticus 20:9

7. Negligence of animals that kill Exodus 21:28

8. Witchcraft Exodus 22:18

9. Bestiality Exodus 22:19; Leviticus 18:23-29;
   Leviticus   20:15

10. Idolatry Exodus 22:18

11. Making Holy annointing oil Exodus 30:33

12. Putting Holy anointing oil on strangers Exodus 30:33

13. Making Holy perfume Exodus 30:38

14. Defying Sabbath Exodus 3:14

15. Working on Sabbath Exodus 35:2

16. Eating flesh of Peace Offerings in uncleanness
    Leviticus   7:20-21

17. Eating fat of sacrifices Leviticus 7:25

18. Killing sacrifices other than at the door of tabernacle
    Leviticus 17:1-9

19. Eating blood   Leviticus 17:10-14

20. Incest Leviticus 18:6-29; 20:11-22

21. Eating Sacrifices at the wrong time Leviticus 19:5-8

22. Consecration of children to idols Leviticus 20:1-5

23. Spiritualism Leviticus 20:6

24. Adultery Leviticus 2:10   Deuteronomy 22:22-30

25. Sodomy/ Homosexuality Leviticus 20:13

26. Relation with a menstrous woman Leviticus 20:18

27. Whoredom Leviticus 21:9 Deuteronomy 22:21-22

28. Sacrilege Leviticus 22:23

29. Refusing to fast on Day of Atonement Leviticus 23:29

30. Working on Day of Atonement Leviticus 23:30

31. Blasphemy Leviticus 24:11-16

32. Failure to keep Passover Numbers 9:13

33. Presumptuous Numbers 15:30-31

34. Gathering firewood on Sabbath Num 15:32,36

35. Failing to purify self before worship Num19:13,20

36. False prophecy Deuteronomy 13:1-18

37. Leading men away from God Deuteronomy 13:6-18

38. Stubbornness and rebellion Deuteronomy 21:18-22

39. Gluttony Deuteronomy 21:20-23

40. Drunkedness Deuteronomy 21:20-23

41. Backbiting Deuteronomy 17:27

42. False dreams/ visions Deuteronomy 13:1-18

Praise God for Christ who has made atonement for our sins
at the Cross. Because there is no way for anyone of us to
keep from sinning. He took our punishment, and gave us a
free pardon. He repaired the damage that sin caused.
He freed us from the penalty of sin and brought us into
relationship with Himself when we accept His sacrifice in
our place.

Kill It!!
{10/8/2002}

Philippians 3:3
"... rejoice in Christ Jesus and have no confidence in the flesh.."

Philippians 3:7-14
"...count all things as loss for the excellence of the knowledge of Christ.
"count them as rubbish <trash; scraps to throw away> to gain Christ."

Nothing compares to knowing Christ!

Philppians 3:16 "...to the degree that we have already attained, let us walk by that."

In other words, walk in the knowledge and maturity in Christ that you already have and trust Him to grow you further in knowledge and maturity.

Walk in what you already have!

Galatians 2:20
"We are crucified <killed, dead> with Christ
dead to everything else except Christ and what He represents.
The old man is dead, so is his attitudes and behaviors
We are raised to new life, a new person in Christ!
New behaviors, desires. Stop trying to just 'clean up' the outside
get Jesus on the inside! He will transform you with His Power.
we must PUT OFF <rid ourselves completely of> old man's
ways. {daily things are either dying or being added}.
PUT ON <clothe ourselves in Christ's spiritual robe of
practical righteousness>.

We must MORTIFY <put to death quickly> the old nature.
The flesh must be nailed to the Cross with Christ.
Colossians 3

Put to death <stop it; get rid of; don't do it anymore>
anger, wrath, malice,filthy language; lies; evil desires; greed;
 fornication; adultery; idolatry etc.

PUT ON <add to your life, start doing>
humility; love; kindness; compassion; mercy; meekness;
patience; forgiveness; obedience; holiness etc.
Focus our interests and ambitions Heavenward.
Cultivating Godly virtues. Jesus changes our 'want to'.
Conform to Christ and press on!
Philippians 3:12-14
".. lay hold of that, which Christ Jesus also laid hold of you".
<Grab hold of, reach for> that purpose and reason that Christ
 called and grabbed hold of you!
There's a reason why Christ called you.
 We must voluntarily choose to do right!
**We never break God's law or change it. It is forever firm
we just bloody ourselves as we hit up against it in
  disobedience and rebellion !

Standing In The Gap

{7/24/2001}

Ezekiel 22:30

"So I sought for a man among them who would make a wall & stand in the gap before Me, on behalf of the land, that I should not destroy it, but I found no one!"

God expects us to 'stand in the gap' for others until they are strong enough to stand for themselves. ~~ Who is standing for you?~~

"Standing in the gap" for family, & friends puts a road block on their pathway to hell!

Ezekiel 3:23-24

"So I arose & went out into the plain & behold the glory of the Lord stood there....& I fell on my face! Then the Spirit entered me & set me on my feet & spoke to me

"Go, shut yourself inside your house"... <prayer closet?>

When He came out, God told him what to say to them. Ezekiel was a watchman to warn them. Ezekiel ch. 2

Start standing in the gap for yourself & others. Stay in God's Word, believe it & put action to your belief.

Ezekiel 22:30 is the 'challenge'!

Acts 16:31 is the 'promise'!

"and they said, believe, on the Lord Jesus Christ & thou shall be saved & thy house".

Acts 2:39

"For the promise is unto you & to your children & to all that are afar off even as many as the Lord, our God, shall call.

Claim your family, friends for Jesus. Stand in the gap for

them.

Just like Rahab in Joshua 6:17. She was saved & her household.

She dared to believe for herself & all she had.

Jericho's walls fell because Israelites dared to believe & take God at His Word & the walls came down!

Joshua 6:16.

Ephesians 4:31-32

What walls do you need to fall?

** walls of indifference?

** walls of anger/ bitterness?

**walls of resentment?

**walls of hate?

Let Jesus deliver you.

You can't give what you don't have. Accept Jesus as Savior & Lord repent of sins, then as He delivers you, bring deliverance to others by 'standing in the gap'.

Jesus bridged the gap! He is the Repairer of the Breach!
Isaiah 58:12.
Nehemiah 4:6-8
The walls were being restored because the people had a mind to work.
Gaps were closed in the wall because the people joined together in unity. The enemies tried to attack & create confusion to stop
God's plans. Unity & restoration scares Satan!
Satan isn't bothered by casual Christianity, if we stay in the boat.
But when we decide to get out of the boat, stepping out on faith Satan takes notice! He gets scared. But keep focused on Jesus believe & apply His Word. The waves will come but don't get back in the boat!
There's security, peace & safety in the boat but you can't go back if Jesus calls you! He will help you! Isaiah 41:9-13.
Satan is afraid of your calling! He is more afraid of Jesus in you so don't be afraid of him!

Steps to Standing In The Gap..
1. Forgiveness..... Jesus forgives us so we must forgive & ask others to forgive us.
2. Declare to Satan.... you can't have my family! Boldly & openly declare God's Word & demand Satan to get OUT! Boldly claim Acts 16:31; Acts 2:39 as well as many other verse. Stand on the Word!   Demand him to get his hands off your family!

Thank Jesus &
Praise Him for what He is doing & will do.
Genesis 19.. Abraham stood in the gap for Lot.
3. Covenant with God ..to never give up until your loved
   ones are saved, healed, & delivered. Pray for them!
As you stand in the gap.. something good will happen
because of it.
They can't get around your road block of prayer. By faith
start seeing them 'saved'. Start believing all the prayers are
answered even if you don't see the answers yet. Thank &
praise Jesus ahead of time.
Because He is working on your behalf in their lives, as you
ask Him to do it, just believe He is working!
In spite of every outward sign. In spite of the appearance of
them lost.
**Don't pay attention, to what you 'see'. Stand & believe by
faith God promises to see them saved. Make up your mind,
no matter how impossible it seems or unrealistic it looks.
Stand up to the devil! Don't believe his lies! Stand on
God's Word.
Stand in the gap!
Stand firm in your faith!
Stand victorius~~
~~you & your household shall be saved...Praise Jesus!

Altar Of Memorial....Ancient Landmarks.
{6/12/2001}

Joshua 4:1-24

v6 " That this may be a sign among you when your children ask in time to come, saying, "What do these stones mean to you?"

v7 " And these stones shall be for a memorial to the children of Israel forever".

<Hab. 2:2-4; Ex. 17:14-16; Pro. 22:27>

12 stones out of the Jordan River & set up at Gilgal

12 stones set up in midst of Jordan River.

These stones were a memorial, a reminder, an old landmark

Pro. 22:27

Don't remove the ancient landmark which your fathers have set.

They were to remind future generations what God has done.

{In the New Testament, the Lord's Supper is a memorial also.}

Each priest carried a stone...which would be a 'personal experience' for them which will remind them of God's provision for them everytime they think about it.

Ex. 17:14

"Then the Lord said to Moses, 'write this for a memorial in the book..."

Hab. 2:1-4

Then the Lord answered me & said "write the vision & make it plain on tablets that he may run who reads it"

Share it also by authority.

Make it clear to yourself...imprint it on your mind, so you will be able to transmit it to future generations & notify those in distant lands.

God has written His plans plainly to use who understand & it's published with authority, you can stand firm on the Word.

It's Truth has been preserved throughout history. It's a 'sure word' & a 'firm foundation'. We don't have to be afraid to tell it because God in all His Authority backs it up!

Our personal experiences are 'landmarks'. Journaling your experiences is a great way to record what God has done.

Also it reminds us of God's provision for us, as we remember those things from the past.

No one can take your personal experiences away.

The Bible is our 'Landmark'. Our pathway that leads us to God.

We can't physically go see the 'old' landmarks that Joshua & others left. Some might go to the Holy Land & see ruins but not all of us can do that. But we don't have to, all the landmarks we need are written down for us in the Bible.

Landmarks help us find our way so we won't get lost.

Makes our way clear.

Altars of memorials are what we look back to & remember what God has done in our lives. Makes our faith stronger to look back & see what He has done for us.

God has a purpose & plan for each one of us, but Satan comes, to 'kill, steal & destroy'. John 10:10

Our own sin nature & Satan's attacks cause us to be distracted from God's purpose & plan for us. Sin & Satan cause us to choose wrong choices which puts us on the wrong road.

We must turn around 'repent', accept Jesus as Savior &
get into His Word so we can follow Him back
to His original pathway for us. Then we can
fulfill His original purpose for us. Jesus doesn't want us side
tracked by sin, or our lives ruined but once we've messed
up we must recognize it & confess it to Him then let Him
help us to get back on the right road.
Even in prison, Jesus can bring freedom, you can start over.
No one decides to one day become a drug addict or a thief or
you name your sin, that wasn't our childhood dream. But sin
happened & along the way we got lost.
Jesus wants to restore us to our Godly purpose, to give us the
abundant life. There's hope in Jesus, it's never too late.
We've never gone too far that He can't reach us.
He loves us that much!
We are all 'prisoners' in bondage to sin, but Jesus sets us free.
John 3:16.
Some Spiritual Landmarks...
Proverbs 7:3
'bind them on your fingers, write them on the tablet of your
heart'. Hebrews 8:10
'For this is the covenant that I will make with the house of
Israel after those days, says the Lord.
I will put My laws in their mind & write them on their hearts
& I will be their God & they shall be my people.'
Hebrews 10:16
'This is the covenant that I will make with them after those
days says the Lord. I will put My laws into their hearts & in
their minds I will write them.'
Now we have the Truth of God's Word in our hearts & minds

which is a clearer reminder to us of what God has done.
We still need the old landmarks but they just confirm
testimony & personal experiences we have with Him.
It's a more sure word, because we personally experience
these things that others have told us about, it makes us
stronger in faith once we know....we know! No doubt!!
Landmarks help us find our way like a roadmap.
**God has a specific plan for our lives & a specific way &
time to bring it to pass!
**At salvation, we are captured by Christ, then He wants
us to be conquered by Christ.
Humble yourself, submit & surrender all to Christ, like the
Alabaster Box, Mary broke at His feet, it's the breaking of
our flesh & it's broken by experiences.
When taking a trip you read the map, watch for signs,
familiar landmarks. If you take a wrong turn, & can't find
your way you can stop & ask people along the path for help
& directions, to help you get back into the right direction.
If you do get lost, you can see familiar landmarks to find
your way.
The Bible is our Landmark, our Roadmap, inside its pages,
tells us what path to follow & what raod to take.
How to turn around & to down the correct path.
If you have strayed, & gotten lost on the wrong road
other Christians who've gone before can help us
Proverbs 6:21-23.
What do the old landmarks mean to you?
When your family asks you what all this means, share with
them your testimony, your story, your history.
Just like priests that each laid down a stone for the memorial
in Joshua 4.

It meant something to them, it was personal, they were able to tell others why it was important.

Jesus paid our price for our freedom, He purchased our pardon with freedom there's great responsibility & deep gratitude.

Freedom is not free, it comes with a high price.

We determine it's value.

There are 168 hours in a week, how much time will we give Jesus.. a tithe of time = 16 hours. It's a good place to start.

Horns Of The Altar
{10/9/2001}

Psalm 118:27

"God is the Lord & He has given us light, Bind the sacrifice with cords [represents Christ's blood].   to the horns of the altar.

 Matthew Henry commentary says...

"The Brazen Altar is a type of Christ, dying to make atonement for our sins. Christ sanctified Himself for His church & as our Altar,

He sanctifies us. In Old Testament days, sinners fled to the 'horns' of the altar for refuge & safety; by virtue of the sacrifice that was offered there. <The sacrifice made atonement for the sin, that made them run to the altar in the first place.> Sanctify = set apart; for God's use.

Horns = power

Jesus' sacrifice has the power to save us!

Jesus' blood is the scarlet 'cord' that runs through the Bible. As we 'grab' hold of Jesus & His sacrifice on the 'altar' the Cross in salvation, we grab hold of His atoning power & we find forgiveness, safety & refuge.

{Colossians 3:10; 1 Kings 22:11; Psalm 75:10;
 Leviticus 23:4-8;
 1 Corinthians 5:7}

 Jesus was bound to the Cross & shed His blood for us. Once we are saved, we need to go 'deeper' in Him, to 'bind' ourselves to Him, offer Him our sacrifices of repentance & brokenness, daily becoming living sacrifices of prayer

& praise to Him.
{Joshua 2:17-21; Isaiah 1:18; Ecc. 4:12; Jeremiah 17:2; Psalm 40:6-8; Hebrews 10:5-10}
Romans 12:1
"I beseech you, therefore, brethren by the mercies of God that you present your bodies a living sacrifice, holy, acceptable to God which is your reasonable service."
{James 1:21; Psalm 51:17; Psalm 34:18}
We must die daily because without dying to the flesh, we can't see His face & glory. Because no flesh can see His glory & live.
We must kill our will & accept His.
We must be humble, & have a broken contrite heart.
Hebrews 12:1.... 'lay aside the sin that so easily besets us.
Remove all prideful attitudes that you won't deceive yourself into thinking you're ok when you're not.
We must have a 'soft' heart that Jesus can mold & shape & write His laws upon it.
We must not 'harden' our heart like Pharoah.
How do we harden our heart?
1. Exodus 7:22.. whenever we think we can do it alone
2. Exodus 8:15; Exodus 9:34... Whenever we pray, for help then when relief comes we fail to do what we promised.
3. Exodus 8:19.. whenever we see God's power & authority, then deny His ability to do miracles today. {being deceived by sin}.
Hebrews 3:13-15.
4. Deuteronomy 15:7.. whenever we have the opportunity to do good & we don't.

Mark 8:17-18.. whenever we have opportunity to
believe & we refuse.
6. Acts 19:9.. whenever we're confronted with Truth &
we turn away from it or mock, scorn or bock at it.
We provoke God by not embracing Truth, or living by
it or only coming to Him in a crisis!
{2 Corinthians 3:14; Proverbs 28:14}
Jesus takes away the 'hard' heart & replaces it with a heart
softened by Him.
God will never harden a heart that wants to be soft.
He wants to mold & shape us. He is the Potter, we are the
clay.
The Potter has the absolute right to do whatever He pleases
with the clay.
He will 'create a clean heart' in us as we believe & obey
Him, as we submit to Him.
Your heart will never be the same again!

Woe To Shepherds

Ezekiel 34

v2-3 "woe to shepherds.... feeding themselves but do not feed the flock."

Matthew 18:11-14

v11 'For the Son of Man has come to save that which was lost...'

Ezekiel 34:4 problems....

the weak not strengthened

sick not healed

broken not bound up

those driven away, not brought back

lost not sought after!

Sheep were scattered

these shepherds ruled with force & cruelty.

The sheep wandered

*no one was seeking or searching for them

* Jesus came to seek & save the lost.

Ezekiel 34:10

the Lord will cause the shepherds to stop feeding themselves He is against them. He will stop them from feeding the sheep which they are not doing anyway He will take their position from them.

Ezekiel 34:11

Lord Himself will search for His sheep & seek them out.

Ezekiel 34:12

as a good Shepherd, He seeks & searches for the sheep to deliver them from all the places where they were scattered.

Ezekiel 34:13
I will bring them out...
gather them
bring them to their own land {fulfilled 1948 Israel}
Ezekiel 34:14-16
I will feed them   make them lie down in rest . seek
the lost bring them back bind up the broken
strengthen / heal the sick
but destroy the fat & strong & feed them in judgment
Ezekiel 34:17-21
Christ will judge between the sheep & the sheep to see
who is of His flock.
He will judge between the fat & lean sheep
among those pushed aside as weak
Ezekiel 34:22-30
I will save my flock!
I will be the one Shepherd over them
in a covenant of peace
I will shower them with blessings
food, safety, deliverance, freedom
they will KNOW that I the Lord, their God, I am among
them they, the House of Israel are My people says the
Lord.
I Am the Good Shepherd.

Transformed By Trouble
{purpose behind problems}

Psalm 119:67 'Before I was afflicted, I went astray but now I keep Your Word.'

Psalm 119:71 'It is good for me that I have been afflicted that I may learn Your Statues.'

Psalm 119:74-75 'Those who fear You will be glad when they see me, because I have hoped in Your Word.'

Romans 8:28 'For we know that all things work together for good to those who love God, to those who are the called according to His Purpose'.

Everything God allows to happen in Your life is permitted for His purpose. What is that purpose? To transform you into the image of His Son, Jesus. To build Christ like character.

Since Jesus being perfect, suffered...we will too.

Hebrews 5:8 'Though He was a Son, yet He learned obedience by the things which He suffered.'

Romans 8:18 'For I consider that the sufferings of this present time are not worthy to be compared with the glory which shall be revealed in us.'

Ecc. 3 To everything thre is a season, a purpose under Heaven.'

Job 5:17-18 'Behold, happy is the man, whom God corrects, therefore do not despise the chastening of the Almighty for He bruises but He binds up, He wounds but His hands make whole.'

Job 11:6   'Know therefore that God exacts from you, less than your iniquity deserves.'

Job 12:14   ' If He imprisons a man, there can be no release!'

Job 13:15   ' Though He slay me, yet I will trust Him.'

Job 14:14   '...all the days of my hard service I will wait...until my change comes'.

Job 42:1-5   'Then Job answered the Lord & said, ' I know that You can do everything. & that no purpose of Yours can be withheld from You. You asked, 'who is this who hides counsel without knowledge?' 'Therefore I have uttered what I did not understand, things too wonderful for me, which I did not know. Listen, please, & let me speak, You said, 'I will question you & you shall answer Me.''I have heard of You by the hearing of the ear, but now, my eyes see You!! Therefore, I abhor myself, & repent in dust & ashes.'

Proverbs 10:17 'He who keeps instruction is in the way of life. But he who refuses correction goes astray'.

Hebrews chapters 11-12 'Great cloud of witnesses'

Remember, no matter how much suffering we go through in life, there are others who have suffered more!

Hebrews 12:4 ' You have not resisted to bloodshed striving against sin'.

Jesus suffered & we will suffer. Focus your eyes on Jesus & not the problems. Jesus said in John 16:33 ' These things I have spoken to you, that in Me, you mayhave peace. In the world, you will have tribulation, but be of good cheer I have overcome the world'.

Troubles comes because of our own sinful choices,
that have consequences but they also come because of the
evil world we live in.
Everyone suffers one way or another. But Jesus has
delivered us from this on the Cross..& He is coming
back soon.

Ashes & Incense

Ashes = used in mourning to show joy had perished.
Just as we are sorrowful for our sins.
Isaiah 61:3
" To console all those who mourn in Zion,
to give them beauty for ashes; the oil of joy for
mourning.
<Jesus will restore our joy>, the garment of praise for the
spirit of heaviness, that they may be called trees of
righteousness, the planting of the Lord that He may be
glorified."
Job 42:6 "Therefore, I abhor myself & repent in dust &
ashes."
Daniel 9:3
"Then I set my face toward the Lord God to make
request by prayer & supplications with fasting,
sackcloth & ashes".
Sackcloth = a symbol for sorrow, mourning. A rough
garment made of camel & goat hair, worn by mourners.
Jeremiah 31:13
"...I will turn their mourning to joy, will comfort them
& make them rejoice rather than sorrow".
Lamentations 5:15
"The joy of our heart has ceased, our dance has turned
into mourning."
Joel 1:13-14
"...lie all night in sackcloth... fast...cry out to the Lord."
Nehemiah 9:1-3

"Assembled with fasting, sackcloth & dust on heads, confessed sins, read God's word for ¼ of the day, confessed & worshipped the Lord another ¼ of the day

King Hezekiah mourned in sackcloth in Isaiah 37:1, 2 Kings 19:1.

Jacob mourned many days for his son in Genesis 37:34.

Exodus 31:11

"...anointing oil & sweet incense for the holy place..."

Exodus 39:38

"the gold altar, anointing oil & the sweet incense...."

Genesis 8:21

"Lord smelled a soothing aroma..."

Exodus 30:1

Altar of Incense was placed in Holy Place before the veil that covered the Most Holy of Holies. Perpetual incense to the Lord throughout their generations. Used upon the Altar of incense.

Exodus 30:34-38

"Equal amounts of sweet spices, stacte, onycha, galbanum & pure frankincense make a compound, salted, pure & holy Beat some of it very fine & put before the Testimony in the tabernacle where the Lord meets with you.

It shall be Most Holy to you. Don't make any for yourself, it's Holy to the Lord. Whoever makes it to smell it shall be cut off from his people!"

Revelation 5:8

"... golden bowls full of incense which are the prayers of the saints."   Revelation 8:3-4

Then another angel, having a golden censer came & stood at the altar {Altar of Incense}.

He was given much incense
that he should offer it with the prayers of all the saints
upon the Golden Altar which was before the throne,
& the smoke of the incense with the prayers of the
saints ascended before God from the angel's hand."
Malachi 1:11
"in every place incense shall be offered to My Name."
2 Corinthians 2:15
"...we are the fragrance of Christ."
Ephesians 5:2
"walk in love as Christ has loved us & given Himself
for us an offering & a sacrifice to God for a sweet
smelling aroma."
Esther 2:12
"Preparing to meet the King, Esther prepared herself
12 months, 6 months with oil of myrrh; 6 months with
perfumes for beautifying women."
Luke 1:9-11
"Zacharias stood at the Altar of Incense in his priesthood
duties while people prayed outside at the hour of incense,
when the angel of the Lord appeared telling him his
prayer was heard."
While we pray our prayers go up to Christ, as a sweet
smelling aroma.
Just like in the temple, sacrifices were burned on the
brazen altar & the ashes represented our sorrow for sins.
When we mourn for our sins & confess & repent, praying
to Christ He sees our 'ashes' & smells our incense as He
hears our prayers.

Our ashes & incense are a sweet smelling sacrifice to Him.
Then He turns our ashes into joy.
Answers our prayers, as He smells the sweet aroma
offered to Him.
Just as the incense was to go up continually from the altar
so is our prayers to be continually before Him.
Psalm 56:8
He puts our tears in a bottle.
Just as He saves our tears, our prayers are stored up in
golden bowls in Heaven with the incense from the altar.
Christ sees every tear of mourning we shed, He sees our
sorrows, He collects our tears, He hears all our prayers. He
smells the sweet aroma as they rise up to Him. He answers
us & turns our mourning into joy.

Jesus Christ The One & Only Savior

In Genesis 3:15 " I will put enmity between your seed &'her' Seed; He shall bruise your head & you shall bruise his heel."
 Only Jesus Christ was born 'Seed of the Woman'.. everyone else is born from man's seed. Jesus had no earthly father.
God the Father through His Holy Spirit entered virgin Mary & she conceived.
 Consider these amazing facts...
 Noah.. had 3 sons, God eliminated 2/3 of all of Noah's decendants.
 Shem.. among his many decendants God rules out all except for Abraham.. now Abraham had 8 children, God completely eliminated 7/8 of all his decendant's except for Isaac who had 2 sons, God eliminated 50% of all his decendants except for Jacob who had 12 sons, God eliminated 11/12 of all those family lines except for Judah Genesis 49:8-12. Generations continued in the tribe of Judah until Jesse.. who had 8 children, God eliminated 7/8 of all his decendants until David ..
 Zechariah 12:9. continuing in his generations Joseph who married Mary the mother of Jesus Christ.
 Where?
Micah 5:2 "But you, Bethlehem Ephrathah, though you are little among the thousands of Judah, yet out of you shall come forth to Me, the One, to be Ruler in Israel, whose goings forth are from of old, from everlasting".

God totally ruled out every other city in the world when He named this specific city! Written 700 years before Christ was born!

When?

Malachi 3:1 " Behold, I send My messenger & he will prepare the way before Me, & the Lord whom you seek will suddenly come to His temple even the Messenger of the covenant in whom you delight.

Behold His is coming says the Lord of Hosts."

The temple was destroyed in 70AD..this prophecy tells us the Messiah would come to the temple so He would fulfill this prophecy.

Who & What price?

Judas betrayed Him for 30 pieces of silver.

Psalm 41:9 "Even My own familiar friend in whom I trusted, who ate My bread has lifted up his heel against Me"

Zechariah 11:12 "Then I said to them, 'If it is agreeable to you, give me my wages, & if not, refrain.'

So they weighed out for my wages 30 pieces of silver".

Matthew 26:13-15; Mark 14:10

God narrows and narrows the prophecies concerning His Messiah until all Scriptures point to One Person.

.Jesus Christ.

Psalm 22 written 1010bc details Jesus' crucifixition 1010 years before He was ever born! Crucifixition wasn't even started until 400 years later!

Isaiah 53 written 700bc also gives us great details, 700 years before He was born!

God is telling us and asking us 'who will believe our
report?'
Many people want to know who the real Christ is.
Who should they believe in. God is pointing down
through all of history...down to One person,,
Jesus Christ!
When other false teachers say that anyone else
is the Messiah you can know they are 1000% wrong
because now you know Jesus Christ is the Only One
who fullfilled all the prophecies
concerning the Messiah.
You can trust Him with your life.
He is the only One & you like the 12 apostles & the
millions of martyers since then can stake your life
on Jesus.
He is worth dying for & millions have. They would
not do that for a lie.
Jesus Christ is asking you...believe in Me?
I AM THAT I AM
I AM your Savior & Lord, your King of Kings & there
is no one else ! Praise the Lord.

Living Sacrifices
"Consecration"

Consecration: to be holy, to make clean, an outward sign of sanctification.

Sacrifices must first be prepared. Entirely surrendered to God.

Completely consumed, devoted to God.

Christ completely surrendered Himself as a 'burnt offering' to redeem us.

He willing offered Himself unto death, a complete surrender.

This symbolizes our entire surrender to God; our sanctification of our whole self. Consecration of a lifestyle pleasing to God.

In Old Testament times, the animals sacrificed were examples of Christ coming as our substitute, sacrificed for our sins, paying our debt. This is a picture of God's redeeming character.

** young ox: His patient endurance as Savior

 1 Corinthians 9:9-10; Isaiah 52:13-15; Philippians 2:5-8

** sheep/ram: Christ's unresisting abandonment to death

 Isaiah 53:7

**goat: sinner or Christ as He was numbered with the

transgressors.

**turtledoves/ pigeon: mourning, innocence, poverty
Isaiah 38:4; Hebrews 7:26; Leviticus 5:7

He became poor so we could become rich. 2 Corinthians
8:9; Philippians 2:6-8.

Priests had to be consecrated before they could serve
God in the Temple. They had to wash their entire body,
symbolizing purifying of the priestly garments. Leviticus
8:22-36..

They remained in the Temple for 7 days while being
consecrated.

A bull was killed for a sin offering; a ram was killed for
a burnt offering; & a second ram killed for a
consecration offering.

The blood was put on the Horns of the Altar, around the
base of the altar. Then the blood was put on the tip of
Aaron's & son's right ear, right thumb & right big toe.
There is no consecration, no redemption without the
shedding of blood. They also took the fat & kidney's &
right thigh along with unleavened bread, used them as a
'wave offering' to God.

Then burnt it all on the altar as a sweet smelling aroma to
the Lord.

After their 7 days of consecration, on the 8th day they were
able to start their service to the Lord in the Temple.

The Priestly Garments...

TUNIC... atones for killing.

PANTS...atones for sexual transgressions.

TURBAN...atones for haughtiness.

BELT...atones for sins of the heart/ impure thoughts.

BREASTPLATE...atones for errors in judgment.
EPHOD...atones for idolatry.
ROBE...atones for evil speech.
HIGH PRIEST CROWN...atones for arrogrance.
Each set of garments were tailored to fit each priest.
If their garments became torn or soiled their service was INVALID!
Those torn or soiled garments were shredded & used as wicks for the oil lamps. The old garments of the High Priest were not destroyed, but hidden so no one could ever use them again!
3 Categories of High Priest Garments..
**Golden garments..consist of 8 garments worn all year round:
ephod, breastplate, robe, tunic, turban, belt, crown, pants
**White garments worn only on Day of Atonement & never worn again: tunic, pants, turban, belt.
**Ordinary garments: worn by all priest's, tunic, pants, turban, belt.
They were made with gold/ sky blue wool/ dark red wool/ crimson wool & twisted linen.
The pants..conceal nakedness of flesh / represents holiness.
The tunic .. covers whole body/ represents integrity/ blameless /righteousness.
The turban...represents character.
The robe.. represents spiritual integrity/ character
The belt...represents a sign of service/ a servant
The ephod/ breastplate..represents reconciling mediator for people of God., a burden bearer, to intercded to God

for the people.

The crown... represents holiness to Jehovah/ Holy to the Lord.

On the end of the tunic were bells, pomegranates & fringe
pomegranates showed divine law/ spiritual food
fringe showed direct approach to God only clad in robe of God's word as the divine testimony on which the convenant & fellowship with the Lord is based.

To remind priest's of calling of God to be His representative.

The Lord calls us to be Living Sacrifices Romans 12:1-2
He has not called all of us to sacrifice unto death like in some countries.

But He wants us to kill our flesh so that He can use us as a Holy vessel in His service.

So we can be His Holy Temple, a clean acceptable place for Him to live. That we can have direct access to His Throne, we don't need another priest, to access God for us. We are now 'priests' who can directly enter His Throne Room through prayer, but we must keep our Holy Garments clean & undefiled by sin.

Then He can make us into the shofar He wants us to be so we can sound His praises anywhere & everywhere at the time He tells us to, making the right sound, because we can only blow our shofar in our own unique way.

No one else can sing our praises or tell our story.

No one else can blow our shofar like we can.

Are you blowing your shofar? Is your trumpet broken or tarnished or just unused.

Offer yourself a living sacrifice to Him & let Him shape
& pressure you & rub off your rough edges..so you can
again sing praises unto Him, & make your beautiful sound
He created you for. We are all His musical instruments but
just like an orchestra we all can't make the same sound, or it
would be just noise but when we come together making our
own sounds, what a pleasing song to the Lord, how He loves
worship & He inhabits the praise & worship of His people,
so sing...sing loud and long!

Pondering devotionals /Bible studies
were part of our studies we have
done in my weekly Prison Ministry
I do with female offenders.
Each one was shared with the women
as part of our study in the Word over
these 17 years of prison ministry work.

Hope you enjoy them as much as they did
each one came as the Lord directed.

It is an honor to share them here with you.

For further contact,
email: lindaprisonmentor@gmail.com

Linda O'Dell
PO Box 593
Harrah, OK 73045

70177041R00029

Made in the USA
Columbia, SC
20 August 2019